Positivity
Or
Electricity

By Janet Novitski

FORWARD

A picture is worth a thousand words. That saying describes a beautiful oil painting of a lighthouse and a boat in the water. The picture is prominently displayed upon entering the door of my office as a reminder of the turbulent waters clients need to navigate in their journey towards calmer waters. That client is the author of this book. The picture was painted by a client after our first visit. The client, who had been an artist, had not picked up her brushes in 23 years as a result of her struggles and the darkness that consumed her. That client is symbol of the resiliency of the human mind and spirit.

The lighthouse has been the symbol of my mission statement *"to offer a safe harbor and guiding light of HOPE to all those who enter my door."* For many of my clients they have lost their compass in life and need a safe harbor, a guiding light, and a non-judgmental place to find their compass and direction in their life and their relationships.

The picture serves as a symbol of my belief in Hope and resiliency of the human mind, body, and spirit to get better. And that lighthouse picture helps me set my compass each time I walk in the office and see it as to why I am still in this field after thirty plus years. Where there is breath of Life there is always HOPE.

Blessings and warm wishes to you all and keep reaching out to get help to find your safe harbor and guiding light of HOPE.

Jan Butterbrodt, MS

LCSW, LMFT, LPC, CSAC

Table of Contents

ABOUT ME

At this point in time, I am a 46 year old woman who has suffered from bipolar disorder most of my adult life. This is my story about bipolar, treatments with electroconvulsive therapy for bipolar disorder, and how my family and friends deal with the procedure and the disease.

I'd like to start by saying that I did my ECT's, electroconvulsive therapy, on a voluntary basis. I was suicidal and medication would not work fast enough for me to remove the hell that surrounded me. I was in darkness that only someone who has experienced depression could even begin to understand. It was not uncommon for me to break out into uncontrollable tears throughout the day, for no reason at all, or snap at family members for no reason, causing them to feel as though they were walking on eggshells around me. It definitely was no walk in the park for them or myself. I definitely did not want to be depressed, nor did I want to cause my family pain. Why did I feel as if the world was trying to suck me into a deep pit? My depression soon turned into suicidal thoughts. My only thoughts were that my family and friends would be better off without me...

I do not claim to be a medical professional. This is my life story and I only give suggestions that have worked for me. At any given time I can become suicidal. This is a story about bipolar and what keeps me alive. I only hope it will help someone else.

Chapter One

I don't know what is worse, the treatment or the disease. Is it worse for the person who is trying to control their disease or the family who tries to hold it all together?

I really didn't notice I had depression of any kind until I had my third son, and even then I just thought it was postpartum depression. I knew nothing about bipolar and didn't for years. I tried to control a rage that literally felt like my blood would burst from my veins, and then, in the next moments, I was happy to be alive. I was a human yoyo and I had no idea what was wrong with me.

I went eight years without a correct diagnosis. I jumped from doctor to doctor, trying over thirty different combinations of medications in twenty years. I was working on my depression and not realizing that extreme highs were just as toxic as extreme lows. What goes up must come down they say. In this case it came down like a meteor crashing to earth.

For years I went to different family doctors and all they said was that I was clinically depressed. I'm not a rocket scientist but even I could figure that one out. I'm not sure they really knew what to do with me, other than prescribing the next new antidepressant. I was depressed and felt helpless. It is not like you wake up one day and say "bipolar, that's it". In fact I didn't even know what bipolar was. They didn't realize that I had *Zippity Do Dah Days*, too! Those were my extremely high days.

It was possible that I had problems even when my second son Erik was born, but I was going thru a divorce soon after his birth. I had just separated from my then husband. I was literally going thru my divorce when Erik was three months old and my oldest son Michael was two years old. Who wouldn't be depressed? I was too busy to notice how depressed I was. All I could do was to charge forward and take care of my kids.

I think you are supposed to be somewhat depressed, right?

There are times when you are depressed and you doing even know it. You are just going through the motions. Numb. Day after, day after day, I was just existing not living. Maybe you aren't very social anymore. At these times you would rather stay home in your pajamas, not even wanting to go out or to work. At this time you become a social outcast. You're a downer and who wants to be with a downer.

Although I was supporting two kids in diapers and working for minimum wage as a hair stylist, I still made it to work. I had to. Who was going to take care of my kids? When you work by appointments, not going to work isn't really an option. Money must be made. Clients are not understanding about rescheduling their appointments. Especially, if you it becomes habitual. You may stop answering phone calls. I know I do. My family can hear the depression in my voice and I get exhausted trying to explain what is wrong. Besides, how could I? I didn't even know. I know I am going through a funk when this happens. Sometimes I would go three to four days without answering my sisters or mothers calls. I would give everyone different ring tones so I could screen my calls from afar. At least then I knew who I was ignoring. I very seldom answered the phone and when I did

I would listen to the person on the other end pleading for an answer. Not caring; just sitting in silence.

With new technology, texting has been a great option on such days. I can let my family know I am ok, just not up to talking. They don't like it but at least they know I am ok. It is better than the "Just snap out of it" lecture I would get. How can you snap out of it? My family understands now, but this wasn't always the case.

I have had to put systems into place for my health as well as the wellbeing of my family. Texting is just one of them. Another would be putting someone else in control of my meds when I was feeling suicidal. I couldn't even trust myself. Sometimes my husband may be in control of my meds for months. Sometimes he is for only weeks.

Even worse you may have a lack of interest in things you once loved, even sex. Hurting the one you love because you can't muster up enough energy to even think about sex. There were times I would sleep on the couch, just to avoid the advances of my husband. I know I was hurting him, but I couldn't help it.

I used to enjoy painting and sketching. I hadn't done this in years. I just didn't feel up to it. I would use excuses as to why I didn't do this anymore. None of them were really good excuses.

There could be a difference in your sleeping pattern. Maybe you sleep all day or go days without a wink. Later, on certain medications, I would sleep up to eighteen hours. I was sleeping my life away so I didn't have to deal with day to day problems. I swear my kids grew up on Disney movies. It was just easier to pop in a movie than to actually entertain them. Movies were a quick fix for a babysitter. I didn't have the energy to teach them or read to them. Add this to the list of things that made me a horrible parent. The list goes on. I was too depressed to care. Maybe I was selfish, but I did all I could to muster up enough energy stay out of bed.

I was so tired. Tired of *"Acting Normal"* all day. I became snappy with the people that were close to me. At least that is a nice way of saying it. You get the idea. But for my husband and kids walking on eggshells was a daily occurrence. I didn't even like to be around myself. This was the key. It was like being duct taped to the hip of the bitchiest person you know, but there is no escape. It is hard to explain how out of control you can feel. Your mind is racing and racing with no end in sight. Your mind can also turn on a dime.

This was true about suicidal thoughts. One minute I was fine and the next I was thinking about how many pills it would take to end it right then. Racing thoughts are very common, especially when your medication wasn't working. Once I got something stuck in my head it was hard for me to do anything until I came up with a solution. This could cause it to be difficult to get to sleep at night. Even stay asleep. My thoughts would keep going over, and over and over in my head. I put a notebook next to my bed in which I could put my thoughts on paper, especially on those nights when I can't get things out of my head. Putting it down on paper sometimes helps but, not always. At least you can try to leave it for a different time.

This reminded me of when I worked for my brother. He would give me an objective to do at work and I would finish it immediately. Again I would get something in my head and couldn't get it out until I had accomplished my task at hand. Or when I told someone to do something, I was inpatient. When I said, "Could you please,_____?" I meant yesterday not next week.

Otherwise I have learned if you can't sleep you might as well get up. Once I got up and tiled the bathroom. It looked great, but I didn't get a wink of sleep. No use getting pissed because the guy next to you is snoring logs. Sometimes I just want to punch them for being able to fall asleep at the drop of a hat. Awful isn't it. It is best to get between 7-8 hours sleep a night. I even go to bed the same time every night; staying on a schedule.

Lack of sleep could easily be one of the signs of mania. It is very difficult to tell someone who is manic that they are manic. Just ask my husband. When you are manic you feel so alive. You feel on top of the world. God like. (Not exaggerating) You also feel like everyone is beneath you, and all the thoughts that keep racing in your head are pure genius. Besides mania is awesome!

Why wouldn't you want to be manic? It is like you are in fast motion and the world is standing still.

My doctor once told me of a patient who was bipolar and addicted to Cocaine. He asked, *"What is a better high, bipolar mania or cocaine?"* She said mania. No wonder so many people are addicted to drugs. I was lucky. I never got into drugs or alcohol. Shopping, that is my drug of choice. I always say,*" I don't need to do drugs, mine are prescribed."*

When I had my downs I still muscled through the day. I would throw my shoulders back, take a deep breath and even though I was in the pits of hell, no one ever knew anything was wrong. My dog could have just died and I wouldn't say anything to my client, but I would smile and act as if it was a beautiful day in the neighborhood. At least that is what I told myself. I just couldn't do it anymore. It took me ten times the effort just to be *"normal"* in appearance; if there is such a thing. No one knew the darkness I was in. That finally backfired. I then became suicidal.

The reason I stopped working for my brother was because I was feeling unappreciated. That was one of the biggest mistakes of my life! My life was my job. After I worked for my brother, I went from job to job; job hopping. I had no problem getting the job, just keeping it. I was a great salesperson. I believe sale's is a transfer of emotion. All I had to do was become excited about the product and I could sell anything.

One employer fired me for being bipolar because they *"didn't know if I would lose it on a client"*. I had more control than that. They were just looking for an excuse to let me go. I knew it was against the law to discriminate but I was unaware of my legal rights at the time. After I was fired I totally 'lost it". This triggered my second breakdown. I was hurt and embarrassed. There was no fight left. I was an empty shell emotionally. I felt as though someone else had control of me and as though I was walking in a fog. By the time I had my wits about me, it was too late to do anything about it legally. It's a shame.

I was working for large weight loss chain and there was a regional manager as well as the manager and assistant manager in the room.   All who witnessed the regional manager say, *" I'm sorry we are going to have to let you go because of the bipolar."* I was in shock. I know I am not the only one who has been judged for being bipolar. This is just something we have to accept. I'm different. I think differently.

At one point I was in the doctor's office crying when they suggested I go on disability. *"Disability? Why? I wasn't any different than anyone else."* I was in shock. I didn't feel like I had a disability. Who did they think they were talking to? It wasn't like I was missing a limb or anything? Doctor after doctor made the same suggestion until I filled out the paperwork and started receiving benefits. It probably didn't help that every time I went to the doctors I was crying. I could help it.

 A flood of emotions engulfed me whenever I had to start over again with new meds or a new doctor. I was looking for help and I was at a loss. It was difficult to even tell them what was wrong. Maybe it is easier to write it down. I felt they didn't understand.

In the mean time I worked on myself by taking my meds the same time every day and making sure I got eight hours of sleep each night. I saw my psychiatrist every six weeks and went to counseling a minimum of every other week. Yeah, right! I didn't do this until I had been on disability for about six years. At this point I had already attempted suicide at least three times and really didn't start the change in myself until I went to the behavioral centers day program. I will explain this later in the book.

I had two visuals that seemed to determine my day. In my mind I kept seeing a picture of a rickety wooden boat with a rope hanging down into the lake. I could see the sun glistening on the water. I could even feel the heat of the sun on my face, but I couldn't reach the rope and I was drowning while trying to reach it. I was being pulled farther and farther away from the rope losing all hope. It may be difficult to understand, but I was living in a hell that no one, other than myself, could save myself from. My thoughts were my worst enemy. I couldn't stop the racing or the negative thoughts. At any given moment I could become suicidal. Later, through therapy, I found that a lot of people in depression see themselves drowning or buried alive. I was amongst the thousands. I was not alone. Nice thought, huh?

A good day was totally different. When I was a young girl I saw the movie "Song of the South". It was a Disney movie. I don't remember a lot of the movie, but I can see the following image. I would drive by a beautiful scenery and visualize an African American man strutting along to the music carrying a fishing pole, with a blue jay on one of his shoulders, singing *Zippity Do Dah Zip a dee yay.* I would feel the sun on my skin and there was a feeling of being grateful to be alive. I loved this feeling. It was like I could feel every breath. Just driving the countryside and seeing the fields of hay could put me into a *"Zippity Do Dah day."*

The medication would help for a while, but then it would stop working. I went from doctor to doctor searching for answers. They all seemed to be as baffled as I was. When on medication I would feel numb, almost like I wasn't allowed to feel emotion. It was like someone was controlling my remote control; following with me crashing into the wall. I missed feeling excitement. Passion. I missed *"feeling"* in general. The side effects were hard to deal with. They consumed me.

There is a reason why so many people with mental disorders don't like to take their medication. I totally understand. I don't take my medication for myself. I take it for my family and friends. It took a long time before I became consistent with my meds because I wanted to feel emotion.

In the beginning I would try a drug and it would take four to eight weeks just to find whether or not it was working. It wasn't. I would go on to the next medication; same thing. Then they would add another medication to the last one trying to get the right dosage. Sometimes they would work for a while, but they said I had medication resistant bipolar. Lucky me! That is why I looked into ECTs.

On one drug I could barely sign my name because the tremors were so bad. I gained almost eighty pounds and lost half of my hair. This was the side effects of just one of the drugs. Believe it or not, at the time I cut hair for a living. The whole time I was trying to control my tremors. Not being very successful. Let's just say they were extremely textured haircuts. Good thing they were in style at the time. I probably shouldn't have been playing with scissors.

No one asks to have a mental illness. Nor should they be chastised for it. Getting help can be one of the hardest things you can do. The first thing, and the most important thing to do, is to admit you have a problem. Just like an alcoholic, drug addict or over-eater, you must admit you have a problem before you can begin to FIX the Problem. There is no other way to get help; and your family and friends can be your support system, but they don't have the answers. Nor should you think they do.

Just getting help can be a struggle. I don't know about where you come from but in my area it can sometimes take up to a year to get in with a doctor. That is why I have had to go inpatient on occasion. Just to get an appointment with a Psychiatrist.

I later learned it wasn't a bad idea to bring someone along to your appointments so they could help you remember any questions or help you answer the questions the doctor asked. I did this on occasion, especially when my meds made me a little loopy. Let's just say that there were times I shouldn't have been driving, let alone going to an appointment that decides your health and well-being. I brought my friend Kathy whenever I could. She usually knew if I was having trouble or not.

Sometimes I was being snappy when my medication wasn't working very well. I may have not noticed a difference but my family and friends did. That is why it is good to have support. You don't have go through this alone. You don't have to be embarrassed. You are suffering from a disease no different than someone suffers from diabetes.

On Lithium I swelled up like I was nine months pregnant, bumped into walls and my speech was slurred. It was like I was a very pregnant Dean Martin, only I was missing the grey hair and the cigarette. Oh, yeah, I couldn't sing either; very attractive.

I had just started on Lithium when I visited my sister Lori in Phoenix. She decided we should go to Laughlin

Nevada. I had no clue where that was, let alone that it was like Arizona's Vegas.

I felt like crap the whole time, but decided to make the best of it. We went to the bar and there were poker machines. I took out a quarter, put it in the slot, and low and behold the sirens go off and I won three hundred bucks! My sister was in disbelief. Even the guy at the bar was shaking his head. I thought it was hilarious. I went back up to the room and lay down for a while.

My skin felt like it was going to burst I was so swollen. In fact, they probably thought I was drunk with my slurred speech and all. I was so dizzy and just needed to lay down. Lori called and told me to meet her by the roulette tables. This is when she decided to teach me roulette. All I cared about was whether it was red or black. But I played a few rounds and won another two hundred bucks. I was up over $500 at the time.

After that I spent most of my time in the room trying to get rid of the water my body decided to take on. It was like my body was a sponge and I was trying to dry it out. Without luck I might add. If only I could have stuck a quarter in me.

When I got back to Green Bay I went to the ER because I couldn't take it anymore. I was so swollen. When I got the results my liver enzymes were high so they took me off of it and gave me some water pills. Lithium used to be the main drug for bipolar so I understood why they tried it on me, it just wasn't for me.

I tried Lamictal a few times. The first time I broke out in a rash on my belly. This was supposed to be a serious side effect. It is a great drug so they tried again, only introducing it to my body slowly. After I was on it a couple of weeks my throat started to close up and I was rushed to the hospital. Just a little side effect when you find out you are allergic. (Sarcasm).

My girlfriend, Kathy, took me to the ER. I even brought all my medication to show them what I was on. Meanwhile, Kathy kept making references to my husband as she held my hand for support, because the nurse thought we were lovers or something. Once they gave me the epi pen the doctor came in to tell me to stop the drug immediately. Are you crazy? You can't stop taking a psychiatric drug cold turkey. They might as well have put me in the looney bin right then. I made an appointment with my Psychiatrist the very next day. He got me in right away and changed the medication. On and on it would go.

I understand these drugs work well for many people. Some people are lucky and find the right combination right away but, for me, it is a guessing game. Your doctor will even tell you. What works for some people may not work for you. I believe in medication for mental illness. I was just looking for something that worked for me. You can't give up. You have to keep going. It can take a while to find the right cocktail. At least that's what I call the concoction of different meds.

The next best thing is to try to keep a sense of humor about things. I know when you are swollen like a balloon you just want to cry, but if you can keep a sense of humor it can be the best thing for you. We tried to keep up the humor when I was going through the ECTs. This helped immensely. We joked a lot and I tried to watch only funny shows and kept the LIFETIME movies away.

Chapter Two

When I look at my husband I can say I am married to my
knight in shining armor. At least that's the way I always
saw him. Yes, he was probably the only knight with a big
thick, porn stache and a mullet, but they say love is
blind. We met when I was working for my brother, at his
salon, and my income was supplemented by government
assistance. So meeting a man who had a job was a blessing.
Around here it was also a fluke. I also did Mary Kay on
the side to try to make ends meet, but I was no way near
getting a new car. By then Erik was one year old and
Michael was three years old. They were my sons from a
previous marriage and basically all I got from the marriage.

Craig has always supported me, even when my medications
were not working, or I went manic. He even dealt with my
dreary days, even when he wanted to run away. Well,
maybe supported is strong word. He tolerated my
behavior. Yeah, that's it. He works two jobs to support us
and has always been my rock. I felt safe in his arms. I
know he had it hard. When he would come home he would
come into the house and tiptoe around me because I would

be sobbing or bitching. You pick. Then he would ask me *"What's wrong?"* All I could say is, *"I don't know."* And I didn't. That's the worst part. The disease would be easier to understand if you knew what was wrong.

I am talking about severe depression, not situational depression. Situational depression could be the loss of a loved one, going through a divorce or losing a job. It can be just as serious, but it is usually temporary.

At the beginning of my illness, I had a great job, beautiful children, a loving husband, and yet I just wanted to curl up into a ball and cry.

When I met Craig I was separated from my ex-husband for about eight months. I was still waiting to finalize my divorce. My ex and I had just moved back to the United States, from Germany, and we couldn't really handle the adjustment. Like a lot of military families, adjusting back into Civilian life is never easy and he couldn't handle the idea of working for a living outside of the military.

My ex-husband was sent to Saudi Arabia during the war called Desert Storm and he came home a different man, even though he didn't see any action. Being in the Military and in a war had changed him a lot. Maybe I should say he wasn't the same boy I had fallen in love with and married. We were very young when we got married. Perhaps we were too young. I'm not sure I had known what love was. I just knew I couldn't handle his temper any longer. I had become afraid of him. Afraid of the man he had become with just cause.

I should say that dealing with my ex-husband didn't exactly go exactly smoothly. I had to have my ex-father in law be our go between just to get anything done. Ray, my ex's father, was great with the kids and would help me whenever I needed him. My ex was so angry and I just couldn't deal with him. When I did separate from him, he threatened me and my family. At that point I wouldn't have been surprised at anything he might do.

He had a gun at his parents' house and I felt he was angry enough to use it. At one point Craig even though my ex out of the house. For some reason he thought that my house was his house. What an idiot.

When we got back to the United States, Michael turned two years of age and Erik was just two months old. It was a struggle at first. I had two little ones in diapers and worked full time working for minimum wage. No matter how you do the math, it doesn't come out at the end of the month. What's that saying, *"There is too much month left at the end money."*

I had a few relationships, if you could call it that, before I met Craig, but there was just something about him that was different. I went out with a couple of girlfriends to mend my heart over a previous relationship and I had started with a couple of drinks before we left my apartment. I have to admit I am a cheap date or should I just say I can't handle my liquor. We would frequent a bar that had cheap shots and darts. Then we would move on to the next bar for a night of dancing. That was our typical night out. Even though we went there often, I never saw Craig there before.

I had a couple of drinks and I told my girlfriend and I wanted to play darts. I was feeling pretty loose that night. There were two guys playing darts and we put our quarters down to play the next round. They asked if we wanted to play doubles. I have to tell you I suck at darts and it was a good thing I had Craig, my now husband as a partner. They were both named Craig. That was easy. I guess he was buying me drinks all night, but I thought I was nursing the same one. I told you, I am not a good drinker. Maybe I'm a little naive, too.

After bar closed we went to breakfast and Craig bought us all breakfast and asked for my number. I never thought he would call, but he called the very next day and we talked for hours.

While going through my divorce, I always had a picture of my two boys on my keychain to weed out the riff raff. Believe me it worked better than you would think. Craig asked me about my boys and said, "*I love kids*", my reply was, *"yeah, right, until you get what you want."* Boy was I wrong. It came to be true. He was great with my sons.

On the night of our first date Craig took me out to dinner and we talked and got along great. When we got home I went to pay the babysitter and he says to me, *"What are you doing?"* I looked at him in confusion and said *"paying the sitter. "* He says, *"Why would you do that, I'm the one who asked you out. If you didn't go out with me you wouldn't need a sitter. "* Let's just say it impressed me.

It didn't take long for me to fall in love with Craig. I had never met anyone like him. I was 25 and he was 29. I had the two boys, but Craig soon treated them like they were his own and we were a family. We had met the end of February and moved in together by Memorial Day. We were engaged by August and married in April. Somehow, when you know you have found the right person, you just know. It may have been a whirlwind relationship but it has lasted over twenty years. We have our ups and downs like any marriage.

Within two weeks after getting married I found out I was pregnant. I did not try to get pregnant and I immediately became depressed. In fact, I was on Norplant, a birth control that is implanted into the upper arm before becoming pregnant. Some say that Norplant can cause depression, so I probably had a double whammy.

Actually I don't even know if depressed is a strong enough word for it. Michael was four years old by now and Erik was two years old when we got married. We had just gotten them potty trained. In fact, Craig is the one who potty trained them both. Now I would have another child in diapers. Here we go again! Just when things were falling into place.

Craig and I never had that *"alone time"* like most honeymooners. It is something I missed. I had really wanted just one weekend to stay in bed and forget about our troubles. I would still like that. Now he is still too busy with work.

Then I thought if I have to be pregnant I might have the girl I always wanted. That thought helped me get through my pregnancy. In fact, all the signs of having a girl were there. My pregnancy was totally different than the previous pregnancies. No such luck. Having another boy just put

me in a downward spiral. I had two boys and I wanted a
girl so badly. I know this sounds shallow, but I am being
honest. I also didn't have a choice in the matter. I'm not
saying I wasn't happy to have another healthy son. I was
very happy when we had a healthy 10 lb. 2 oz. baby boy.

When Brian came home Craig was great with him. I tried
breast feeding the first two weeks, but he was losing weight
and we had to bottle feed him. I was having trouble
bonding with him, and pretty much passed him off to
Craig. If Craig could have, I think he would have breastfed
him. Craig got up in the middle of the night to feed him
even though it was with the bottle. He took him wherever
he went. Even changed his diapers and bathed him. I
pretty much walked away, and my relationship with Brian
has always suffered. From then on Craig always put Brian
first. Maybe he needed to. But our relationship suffered. I
was always the third wheel in my own house.

When we would take a family drive Brian was in the front
while I was in the back with the other boys. Instead of
taking me out, Craig took Brian wherever he went and left
me at home stewing. We went out three times a year, my

birthday, his birthday and our anniversary. I wish I was exaggerating. I'm not. At first I joked about it, but then it just became very painful.

I couldn't believe I allowed such a thing, but I did. It became easier for me just to accept it than to argue about it all the time. When I argue, I just feel like I am being a bitch and he thinks I haven't taken my medication. Whenever they came home from somewhere, all I could feel was a jealousy that would make your head spin. Not only was this hurtful, but a mother should not be jealous of their child. I couldn't help it and it wasn't Brian's fault. It was Craig's and mine for letting it happen. I just wanted to be a part of their lives. I was always shut out and I couldn't get Craig to understand how I was feeling.

Even now, Brian works out of town and calls his father almost daily. I would call and text and try to chat with him on facebook only to find silence. A year ago I cut my hand while making a batch of body butter. The coconut oil was in a container shaped like a milk jug and I tried to cut the lid off. The blade I was using slipped and I cut across the top of my hand and wrist, about 2 and ½ inches, and needed medical attention immediately. I called Brian into the room and showed him my wrist and his reaction was, *"What am I supposed to do about it?"*

About this same time Craig stopped home and he was on his way to deliver some feed to a neighboring farmer. I asked both of them to take me to the hospital but, Brian had plans with friends and wouldn't drive me and Craig decided to go and deliver the feed. I ended up having to drive myself nearly 20 miles to the local Emergency Room. The whole time I was trying to hold the towel on my wrist while driving. I couldn't believe that they both felt so little of me. I had just missed the artery and the doctor told me how lucky I was. Fifteen stitches later I came home. I had wanted their support. I had needed their support.

The location of the cut could have meant another mandatory three day stay at the psych ward because the ER team was afraid I had possibly attempted suicide. I assured them it was an accidental cut and they released me, but only because they had another more serious emergency. After I had Brian, I went to my family doctor because all I did was cry, or I would get so angry that it felt like my body was just going to burst from the blood that was boiling through my veins. I didn't know that anger was a sign of depression. I was afraid to discipline the kids because I was worried I couldn't stop hurting them. There was no stopping the rage once it began. In fact it would intensify. It scared me. I didn't want to hurt my children, nor did I. I wasn't going to put my children through what I had been through as a child. I chose to stop the cycle.

I remember going to the doctor and asking for help and as I left his office I heard him say to one of the nurses, *"That woman is going to jump off Tower Drive Bridge."* I was in disbelief and very depressed. How could a so called medical professional even let me go home if he thought I was that bad. He had no understanding of the helplessness I felt. I was powerless. I should have been sent to the psych ward for help.

As soon as Craig got home from work, I said *"here take the kids"*. Then I would go to a friend's house or to my sister's house just to get away from everything. I left him in charge and took off for a while. He was so good with kids.

But I took advantage of this. I just couldn't handle the responsibility and it was easier to pass the buck.

I still have trouble holding on to a newborn today. And I had three of them. I get anxious and it is hard to control my emotions. My memories haunt me.

It is a terrible feeling when you aren't able to control your thinking. The racing thoughts and the fact that your emotions can turn on a dime and know you know you're being a bitch, but you can't control it. As my husband would say, *"You're being snappy."* I didn't even want to be around myself, but I was trapped. It's like your body is trapped with a mind that won't stop moving, like a freight train.

After a few suicide attempts and several ECT's, I was religious about taking my medications. I learned to take my medication every day at the same time. This kept me more of an even keel. I would hate it when someone would ask, "Did you take your medication?" It is like you are not allowed to have a bad day or bad moment in time. The fact is that if you miss your meds that day it won't affect you until days later. Sometimes I think it is a copout on their part because they use it to try to prove they did nothing wrong. It is easier to blame the mental case.

After a while I started to recognize the symptoms of my mania and depression. I at least became aware of my emotions and could try to counteract the symptoms. Let's just say I learned my triggers. I tried to be prepared for these moments. As long as I was somewhat prepared I could sometimes change the outcome.

After years of going to different family doctors, I still wasn't getting better, so I went to a Psychiatrist. I was lucky I could get in with one. The average time to get in with one is three to six months in our area sometimes longer. When you are that depressed you don't have six months. A lot of times you don't have six days.

I learned rather quickly that family doctors don't deal well with psychiatric drugs and are at a loss with what to do with someone with mental illness. It is still very difficult to admit that I have Mental Illness. It was years before I admitted I had mental illness. It was like I was a failure. I was embarrassed for myself and my family. I didn't want to be labeled.

When I first started having problems I was a hair stylist that specialized in Hair Replacement and worked for my brother. It was great. I loved this job. I was his best salesperson and I worked with people that needed me. When I was manic, I felt like I was a god. I was not only giving them hair but I was changing peoples' lives. I saw clients, who had never dated, do a complete 360 degree change in their lives, have relationships, get married and have kids. I could change someone's life and give them self confidence in just two hours. Yep, I was god like. Sometimes I still feel this way.

I learned that sales were a transfer of emotion and I was very good at it. Some say I could have sold ice to an eskimo.

When I went to my family doctor he put me on Prozac because of the level of anxiety and he felt I had postpartum depression. I couldn't escape myself and within a couple of weeks I had a nervous breakdown, and quit the job I loved.

My brother had gone fishing for a few days. Meanwhile one of the girls I worked with was giving me the cold shoulder. Let's just say this pissed me off, so I went to the appointment book and crossed off my appointments and told them to fuck off. The girl that I worked with got in my way and I just wanted to shove her if not more. She was *'in my space'* and I felt cornered like a trapped animal. I think I could have spun my head around, just like in the Exorcist. I had to get out of there. I glared at her with a look to kill and knew I had scared the shit out of her. She soon backed off. It was probably a good idea if she valued her life.

David's wife called and tried to console me. This is just one of the times I quit working for my brother. It took me about six months to be able to go back to work and maybe I should have waited. I first started out by telemarketing on Sunday nights and then gradually went back to doing hair.

Soon, after I went back to work he opened another store in Appleton. It was more like a satellite shop. Just open a couple days a week to service the clients that were driving to Green Bay. I was the likely choice for commuting since I could do both sales and service. I started out just two days a week in Appleton and then worked in Green Bay the other three days.

When I did hair replacement and sales I excelled at this or maybe I was just manic. When I started in Appleton I must say I read a lot of books at first. Don't tell David, but I watched a lot of movies too. Soon I had to hire someone and eventually we grew and we relocated and hired some more hairstylists. Eventually I was managing a staff and our salon was selected, 7 years in a row, as one of the top 200 Salons in the Nation.

I did so much studying of sales and hair replacement I was unstoppable. I was always reading or listening to Sales tapes to get better. Then David and I participated in a week long sales seminar in Vegas. This was another benefit of the job. We were taught a whole different language. I would sell hair pieces without them even knowing what they had just bought. All I would say is *"We use human hair that is individually attached to a fine membrane. Then we use a surgical type adhesive to keep it in place for three to seven weeks."* I was on fire!

A couple of years later I had an argument with David and quit once again. After I quit my job I cried for weeks. I was out of control. This is one of the times I should have been institutionalized but wasn't. I was left taking care of three kids when I couldn't take care of myself. The only thing I was capable of doing was throwing in a movie for the kids and I ran through the motions by doing only the necessities. They were fed and bathed. That was about the extent of it.

I really don't have many memories of the kids when they were little. Maybe it was because I wasn't there, in my mind, or it could have been the depression that repressed the memories, or even the medications I had been on over the years. It is difficult knowing and dealing with the fact that I will never get those memories back. I miss that.

My husband was so supportive. He was taking care of the kids and the house and working both a full-time and part-time job. He is one of those guys that sticks it out through thick and thin. Believe me I am as surprised as you are. I still don't know why he stays.

I couldn't help feeling my family was embarrassed of me; my parents, my brother, my sister, and worst of all my children. I was so out of control and I hated myself. I continued with the Psychiatrist for about eight years before I was labeled with bipolar. In truth it was Dr. Hunter who diagnosed me. I had met him during a psych evaluation for bariatric surgery. I had told him about my depression, but explained about my *Zippity Do Dah days*. He then labeled me with bipolar. I had no idea what it was.

Chapter 3

There came a time when Craig, who works construction, had been laid off for a while. We didn't have enough money to buy any Christmas presents for any of the kids, let alone three. Later, my uncle's family helped out with a thousand dollar gift card from Walmart. This was after my three day mandatory vacation stay.

Meanwhile, we fought constantly. There was always tension in the air. I couldn't take it anymore and I saw no way out. I was living in the depths of hell and couldn't find a way to surface. When you are in a depression there's a darkness that falls upon you, not knowing if you will ever see the light of day. At this point there wasn't even a glimmer. By this point I was not rational. I felt that Craig and my children would be better off without me. There was nothing they could have done or said, I made up my mind. I could not take the pain any longer.

This was also about the time my oldest son went to live with my ex-husband. My heart was so heavy. I missed him so much, but we had an understanding that when the boys turned 13 they could decide on which of us they wanted to live with. There was nothing I could do.

Michael moved in with his father at age 13. My ex-husband pressured him on and on until he folded. My ex paid $140 a month for 9 years while he worked cash jobs so that he didn't have to pay any more. Basically he was a professional student and went on to school. On and on and on he went to school until he reached a Master's Degree. This schooling helped him keep out of the work force so he didn't have to help support his children. Can we say Deadbeat Father? (Sarcasm)

He finally got a job through which he could have helped support the children but he talked Michael into moving to Chicago with him. This way he had one child and I had one child and he didn't have to pay child support. How convenient. After a few years in Chicago he got a job in Wisconsin and left Michael with his mother to take care of him. It was a game to him. He didn't even take on the responsibility that he had asked for. What a loser.

Not only did Michael go to live with my ex-husband but they moved to Chicago and my ex made it very difficult for me to see him. Any given weekend I would visit Michael, it would cost me around $600 by the time I brought the boys and got a hotel, fed them, and entertained them. It was far between visits and I felt guilty. He would even come to town and not tell me so that I couldn't see Michael then either.

One morning Craig and I had another fight. The fights were happening more often than not. They were usually about money or his drinking problem, my lack of work or the kids. This day it was all of the above. He had been frequenting a bar daily with no consideration for me and the kids. I would call and call and he wouldn't answer his phone. All this time I was worried he was in a ditch or arrested or anything else my mind could think of. He had no idea of the pain I was in or the emptiness I felt. My mind was racing, doing spirals even. Why was he doing this to me? The kids?

By going to the bar he was spending money we couldn't afford to spend. Craig was working only part time. He was laid off every other week. I wasn't currently working. Money was extremely tight. I was depressed even more because the bills were adding up and I could see we were getting behind more and more.

The bitching I was doing wasn't helping but, I couldn't help it. I felt that Craig and the kids would be better off without me. I just wanted out. I wanted to run away. I felt trapped in a life that was sucking the life from me. There was no place I could go; helpless.

That morning I took a little over one hundred Valium tablets and whatever else I could find in the cupboard. I think there was some Codeine too. I would go in the kitchen and take a handful of tablets. Then go in the living room. Back and forth I would go until my girlfriend Kathy called to see if I wanted to go to a movie. I can't believe I answered the phone, let alone agreed to go. It was like being drunk at first. It was like I forgot what I was doing. I wasn't able to think straight. I was in a daze.

I got in the car and drove about 12 miles before I hit the back of a car at a stop light. The ambulance came and all I could do is cry. I kept going in and out of consciousness. My body was numb. I just wanted to die. I was sick of living in a hell that had no way out, at least that's what I thought at the time. I was only conscious enough to say which hospital. The next thing I knew I woke up and they were cutting off my favorite jeans. I was fading in and out.

I arrived at the hospital in the early morning and couldn't keep my eyes open so they kept me under close observation. At that point they knew nothing about the pills I took. They thought it was from the car accident. I woke up several times to see my husband and youngest son there. I was wondering how they found out I was there. I was angry. How dare they call him? He never answered his phone when I called but he answered it when the hospital called?

I think my ex mother in law and ex sister in law came to visit me also. Thank god they didn't bring the kids.

I remember waking up in a ct scan, but remember little else until my cousin Cheryl came to the hospital with a date. Can you believe it. Who would bring a date to something like that? What was she thinking? This was also her first date with the new guy. What an impression. She brings a date to the hospital to see her crazy cousin who just tried to kill herself! (Sarcasm) She shook me awake, and then asked what I took. At the time I was totally unaware of her date until I met him again months later, and was embarrassed to find out he had been there.

"Stuff" I said.

I was pissed. Really this is an understatement. I thought I had finally found a way to make the pain go away and I failed. I can only compare it to a child that was told they were going to Disneyland and then the day comes and you tell them they can't go. I was angry. I was unsuccessful. I had failed. Just add this to my other failures.

I should tell you I am a religious person and suicide is against all my values. I didn't plan my suicide like some people might think. I didn't give away my worldly possessions or even leave a note. I just wanted to end my misery. My mind was my worst enemy. My mind never stopped.

In fact, I believe that a lot of people could rid themselves of the guilt that they could have helped someone before they try suicide as an option. If someone is going to commit suicide there is nothing you can say or do that will stop them. If someone says, *"I'm going to kill myself it is a cry for help or the need for attention."* There is a difference between them and someone who is successful. It was not all that uncommon for suicidal thoughts to just pop in my head. No planning was needed.

Another important thing to remember is the suicidal person is NOT BEING SELFISH. Their mind is in a bad place and they are suffering something the person who has no Mental Illness can ever understand. If the suicidal person was *"in their right mind"* they would never put themselves in a situation of killing themselves or hurting their families in any way. Telling a suicidal person that they have been selfish is very cold and unfeeling and lacking compassion for their situation. No one CHOOSES Mental Illness!

Another one I heard is that suicide is a coward's way out. These are ignorant people. They are not a coward. They are hopeless.

At around 10 pm they finally figured out that I had taken the valium. This was about eleven hours after the accident. I don't know if they took blood work or what happened. Actually I thought I hidden my tracks quite well and no one would ever find out what I had taken but Craig found the empty bottles behind the couch. Who looks behind a couch, anyway? (Sarcasm) He must have went home when Cheryl came to the hospital. What would make him think to look there? I thought no one would ever find them. Believe me, it is not like anyone in our house ever cleaned under the couch. I can't imagine what else he found? Huge dust bunnies?

Cheryl told the nurse what I had done and it was immediately followed by a Charcoal Shake, in which I was told I could drink it or they would shove it down my nose. Let's just say I drank it. It was thick and I gagged as I drank it, but I guess it is better than the alternative. It was so cold; really cold, abnormally cold. I held my breath as I drank it. Well, I chugged it like a cold beer.

The next day they failed to mention that the shake will absorb all of the toxins I took and flush them out. That is if you can make it to the bathroom. Let's just say I was none the wiser when I stood up to go to the bathroom, only I didn't have the opportunity to flush it because it was running down my leg. Nice. (Sarcasm) I bet my cousin was sorry she came to visit me right then. The things that make you close.

I have to say that I did have a hot nurse. It was a guy that looked like Stone Cold from Wrestle Mania. Not bad I must say. I bet he was sorry he made me drink the shake though, since he was on the clean-up committee.

They limited who could call me or come to visit. I really didn't care who called or visited but, I put my brother on the list for no calls or visits. I know this affected our relationship, but I felt I was such a disappointment to him. He was successful and lived a life that I felt looked down on ours. My suicide attempt probably didn't help what he thought of me, and at that time he didn't understand my illness.

I was supposed to lay there and think about what I did. What a joke. Believe me I did think about it. Once again I had failed and I couldn't get the anger out of my system. Anger that they had found me, taken me to a hospital and had SAVED the Life I had tried to destroy.

My parents called which didn't help. I understand their concern, but it wasn't helping. They had been divorced for years and all of a sudden they were in cahoots with each other. They bought me a bible together with the engraving *"Love Mom and Dad"*. It was a wonderful and loving gesture on their part but, it angered me because, at the very least my parents tolerated each other. That was it. And that was on a good day. My whole life it was, *"your mother did this or your father did that."* I was always in the middle.

They could barely speak civilly to each other under normal circumstances. Finding God was not going to help me at the time. I already had, even though some readers may ask how. I was the one who always went to church. It wasn't until I got older that they found God. When I was younger our neighbors brought us to and from church. Our parents wouldn't even go to the church plays or other functions in which I was involved. They always had something better to do.

I was visited by a doctor who put the guilt on me of leaving my children motherless. He must have bitched me out for 15-20 minutes and then left me alone with my thoughts. I wasn't going to listen to him. I had already made up my mind. Nothing he said was going to change that. Later this doctor would be a savior in many ways. I laid there and all I could think about was how my children and husband would be better off without me and how furious I was. I'm sure this is not the reaction they were hoping for. But I think it is common. I have talked with others who had tried to commit suicide and they all said they were angry.

I had a combativeness that was out of my character. I wanted to fight with everyone. By nature I am the pleaser. You know the type. I was always, the one who said yes to whatever was asked of me. It didn't matter what someone said to me I made up my mind life would go on without me and it took weeks, months, maybe years to get it out of my mind. Really the only thing that gave me some relief was the electroconvulsive treatments but, it was actually a couple of years before I got the relief.

The doctor that chewed me out made a big difference in the way I thought about my life and helped me find the resources I needed to change my life for the better. I didn't realize that he was going to be the best psychiatrist I ever had or that I would be forced to seek other help because of insurance. I have to say when I found out that I would have to go to Dr. Hunter I was less than pleased because of our first meeting in my hospital room.

In the meantime, I was given a choice. I could go to the rehabilitation center voluntarily or the police would be nice enough to give me a ride. (Sarcasm) I decided to let Craig take me. He had packed my bag already, so we were off to the center.

I guess I was lucky in a way. When we got the rehab center there was only one room left in the less guarded area. There was a ward in the hospital that you couldn't even wear your bra, in case you get some funny ideas.

I had a mandatory three day stay. Three days is not enough to change your mind about taking your life. Even thirty days wouldn't be enough. Part of the protocol was for Craig to regulate my medication so the temptation wasn't there for me to take another entire bottle. Believe me, the temptation was still there. He had to do this for weeks, always bringing my medication to work with him, so that I wouldn't overdose.

Not only was this hard on Craig and myself, but it was hard on the kids. A nine year old should not have to celebrate his birthday at the mental ward of the hospital. We couldn't even afford to get Brian a present. My brother and his wife took him to Toys R Us to get a few gifts. I was oblivious to this at the time, but very thankful later. All I could give him was one of my crafts that I had made over the past days.

My boys still have the items I made. I think they hold on to them as a reminder. I wish they wouldn't. The guilt of what I have done to my children is something I have never been able to rid myself of. All the therapy in the world wasn't going to change the way I felt about the way I let my children down.

My therapist told me that I couldn't blame myself for what a young mother did. At least the kids did not have to go to a funeral or the morgue. I guess that is one way to think of it. But the negative thoughts still swell within my brain.

While I was in-patient at the hospital they grouped me with the drug addicts and alcoholics. Of which, I am neither. This made me even more angry. I had no sympathy for these people. I kind of had a tough shell at the time.

I lived with an alcoholic. I knew what their families were going through. They were oblivious to what they did to their family, as oblivious as I was about what I had done to mine. I have to say it made me bitter listening to them whine. All the time I was thinking, did they know their family was wondering if they were in the ditch somewhere, in jail, hurt or even dead. After I got out of the hospital I even tried **ALANON,** but it just wasn't for me. I knew I should be more understanding, but it wasn't easy being there and I felt is was a little too ironic.

My psychiatrist started me on light therapy the very next day. He thought this would help with the depression. In fact, I had to get up at 4:30 am to use the light. I am sure that it helped. (Sarcasm). Through October thru March I have a hard time with my depression and being suicidal. Years later my husband would put plant lights all around the house to help with Seasonal Affect Disorder, the Winter Blues. Our own way of light therapy. The only problem with this is that you can become manic if you don't know your signals.

After I left the hospital, it was weeks before I could be allowed to handle my medication or be left alone. I was still suicidal. My sister and my mother called a couple of times a day to check on me, and if I didn't answer I got scolded. I couldn't even pee without being yelled at because if I didn't answer the phone they got worried. I understand they were worried, but I just wanted to be left alone. Maybe I needed to think about what I had done, but they still wouldn't like what I was thinking. I basically slept. I was trying to sleep away my life.

I went a few more years of medication and therapy before I started ECTs. I was never quite right. Somehow that sounds funny. Oh, well. Something was always going wrong with the meds. They even called it medication resistant bipolar, because medication would work for a few months and then they would have to adjust my meds. Either the medication wouldn't work or it would have to be adjusted. I just couldn't win.

Chapter 4

I felt my family didn't realize my difficulties with day to day activities until I had my first ECT series. That is when they started doing some research to understand what I may be going through. Bipolar was still a mystery to them. Up until then they thought I could just snap out of it or all I needed to do was find the Lord and all would be fine. My step mother even tried to pray over me. She thought I had demons and just needed a good exorcism or something. I could tell you what she needs but, that would be in words I don't wish to use right here. (Sarcasm)

I don't remember exactly how I had made the decision for ECT other than my current doctor had suggested it after I had a reaction to Lamictal. I did a lot of research, talked it over with my family members, my dad, my mom, my aunt and my siblings and I knew there could be some short term memory problems but during my first two series, I consider this an understatement.

While my first two series of ECTs were not typical, it became relevant that my doctor that did them was not real ethical. I lost six months previous and six months after the ECTs. All in all I lost three years of memory. My kids were afraid I would forget them. This was really difficult for them.

When Erik found out about the memory loss he called his older brother Michael to tell him. Michael began to cry because he thought I forgot him. This was not the case. I remember my sons and my love for them. I hold them very dear to my heart. They are my world. I remember my childhood the best, but have trouble with my memories after Brian was born.

Instead I had severe short term memory loss. It was like Alzheimer's. I could remember how I met my husband but I couldn't remember him calling me ten minutes before. It was horrible. We soon started using a notebook to remember things and I started keeping a journal. We can thank the movie *Fifty First Dates*. I had to write all my passwords down and any other information that you may not think you would have a problem remembering.

In order for me to get the ECTs the first time, I had to go in-patient; another vacation stay. That was the only way they would do them. They had to do a physical first and I was given an EKG. After several physical tests and blood work, I was ready for my first ECT. ECT is usually administered to patients in a series of treatments, ranging from six to twelve treatments over a two week period. In my case they did 12 treatments over a five week period of time. Then this is followed by monthly maintenance only I never quite made it that far because the Picc line would get infected or I would have an allergic reaction to the adhesive. I started my first series the following Monday.

They woke us at 4:00 am to go to the hospital via short bus. There were anywhere between six to twelve patients at any given time. They also had a few who came in as out-patients. I was able to do this after a while.

"Janet, you can come in now" the nurse said cheerfully. Of course she was happy, she wasn't the one getting the shock treatments. I undressed and put on a peek a boo dress and my free socks with the grippers on the bottom. I should say here that I have a lot of them, blue and brown

socks. What do you do with gripper socks? They never fit in your shoes anyway.

I was asked to go to the bathroom. I guess you lose part of your bodily functions during the procedure. At least they didn't have me do an enema.
The beds were all lined up with a curtain between us. This is so you had privacy. What a joke? Who are they kidding? I wonder if they would have done the ECTs that way if it was one of them. It was very debasing. Embarrassing.

I could hear the treatments being done one after the other, waiting my turn. I could hear the hum of the machine and the patients going in and out of anesthesia. I would hear gurgling noises or moaning. All while waiting my turn. I had an ipod and I would try to turn up the volume to muffle the sound. I would watch the movie *Young Frankenstein.* This probably was not my best choice of movies. Hearing the others getting their ECT's made me very apprehensive, anxious and scared. I would try to catch my breath. Many times I would have an anxiety attack before the ECT.

"Can I get you a warm blanket," the nurse says. Of course I am not going to turn down an extra blanket while I am wearing only a flimsy gown and some ugly gripper socks. If they were really nice, they would have given me a water bottle. But of course we couldn't have anything to eat or drink before the treatment. It reminded me of when I was in labor with my kids. But I didn't even get ice chips.

"I'll be right over to put in your I.V."

"Could you get the anesthesiologist?" I asked. Knowing they would not find a vein. I have had instances that they sent me to the waiting room to drink water just so they could take my blood. Now they wanted to administer an IV without giving me any water. I knew this wasn't going to be good.

"Don't worry we do this all the time. I'm sure I can get it." Oh my God, it was like they were students, one after the other. Again and again they searched for a vein. Four people take their chances with my veins until they finally get the anesthesiologist. By this time they are

looking at the top of my foot. Tears are streaming down my face. And all I can think about is I hope they dry my face before they put the probes on my temples. Finally they put the I.V. in my foot. That is one memory I will never forget. After that I would get anxiety attacks just having people look for a vein. The next day they scheduled me to get a picc line in.

A picc line is a direct line into the vein that stays temporarily in place for people who are getting continual treatment such as chemo. I was a special case, an experiment so to speak. A tube is inserted in the arm that hangs out about four inches from where it is inserted. It is then maneuvered up the vein close to the heart. It can be very dangerous to get air into it so I had to be very careful. And it requires maintenance of injecting a gel like solution into the end. But I had to have my friend Kathy or my husband do that. I'm not complaining because it made my visits a little bit easier. It is very uncommon to have a picc line in for ECT. I am thankful they allowed me to get it. I later got a picc line every series of ECTs. The nurses were of course thankful.

The doctor comes in and he is a beautiful specimen of a man. He was an Egyptian with dark wavy hair and dark eyes that the nurses swoon over. Maybe this won't be so bad. Always wearing a suit and speaking with an accent.

They administer an IV of an anesthetic (i.e. Brevital) in my arm and I am asked to count (I was asked to count backwards) until I become am totally under sedation. As I am counting backwards I taste a metal in my mouth from the anesthesia they use. It is from a little vial.

Then an IV of succinylcholine is put in the arm (relaxing the muscles to prevent broken bones and cracked vertebrae), a rubber block is inserted in the mouth to prevent biting on the tongue. A mask is placed over the mouth so the brain is not deprived of oxygen and conducting jelly is rubbed on the temples and electrodes connected. The jelly is like the stuff they use for ultrasounds. The doctor presses a button and electric current shoots through the brain, causing a grand-mal seizure for 20 seconds with the patient waking within 30 minutes.

"Janet, you're done honey," the nurse speaks softly.

"Do you need help getting dressed?"

I was confused and disoriented. It was like waking up from a deep sleep where you are dreaming you're awake but you can't make your physical body move. I have to say you don't walk very straight afterwards either. Of course you need the assistance of a nurse.

I gradually got my wits about me, but it took several minutes. Meanwhile, my head felt like it was being squeezed in a vise grip and someone kept tightening it to increase the pressure. Every muscle of my body was tight. It was like a charlie horse in the middle of the night. You know, like the kind where your calf becomes the back of your knee. All I kept thinking about was what bus hit me and did they catch the S.O. B.

I continued to run through the motions as the nurse helped me. A toddler getting ready for bed would have been easier to get ready. It was time to leave; I had to get dressed so I wouldn't miss my ride on the short bus back to my luxury accommodations at the rehab center. (Sarcasm)

They lined up all the wheelchairs to bring us to the short bus. The short bus was crowded today there must have been 12 (at least I think there was 12) of us who got up at the crack of dawn to get 450 volts run through our temples with the hope of saving us from the darkness which lives within. Normal people just wake up with Folgers in their cup to get them going but not me though I am hard core.

When I talk about shock treatments, I usually get the same response.

"I didn't think they did those anymore." or my favorite *"aren't they illegal?"*

Most people associate electroshock therapy with torture rather than healing. Like the movie One Flew Over the Cuckoo's Nest. Since the 1980s, this practice has been quietly making a comeback. The number of patients undergoing electroconvulsive therapy, has tripled to 100,000 a year. And the numbers continue to climb today.

ECT's were introduced in the mid-1930s, when scientists discovered that by triggering a seizure, they were able to shock psychiatric patients back into a functioning state of mind. It was designed to be a treatment for curing schizophrenia, but doctors found it also seemed to benefit patients with depression, bipolar disorder and catatonia.

After my treatment I am to rest and go about my normal activity. This meant arts and crafts back at the rehab center. My first project is reminded to me by my brother who told me of the beautiful collage I made with one picture cut out with my round ended scissors. It was glued at a diagonal angle to show my creativity. It is hard to believe I was class artist in high school. This was far from my best work.

Meanwhile, a girl on my floor made a collage that was completely filled on the paper. She ran down the hall to get it just to show my brother. I had to giggle. My brother was definitely out of his comfort zone. But he was kind to the girl.

I have to rely on the words of others to tell part of my story because after all is said and done after my three series of ECTs I am continually learning new things. I lost 3 years of memories that won't come back. Sometimes I get a glimmer, but it just isn't there. So I had to rely on the help of others to jog my memory. Actually they kept my memories for me, for I went blank.

After three treatments as an inpatient and several arts and crafts projects that my son's gladly put on display in their rooms, I was sent home to finish up the 12 part series.

The picc line could not get air in it or get wet so we carefully maneuvered a long blue glove from the farm down the road and a rubber band so I could take a shower. I won't tell you what the men at the farm use these types of gloves for. Suffice it to say it isn't a pleasant experience for the cows. Craig picked up a few from the neighboring farm.

The days blended one into the next. Craig and I would get up at 4:00 to be at the hospital at five to be prepped. After my ECTs were done, my friend Kathy would pick me up. We would then go to the I.V. room to get my picc line flushed and the bandage changed on my arm. Then we would stop at McDonald's on the way home for an Iced Coffee. It became tradition. I think the caffeine helped a little with my head ache.

Kathy said I would ask the same question after every treatment.

"Why am I doing this?"

She would answer me best as she could by saying that my doctor recommended it after lengthy trials of medications and that I researched it and decided to do it. Kathy was a godsend to me and my family. I grew up in a suburb of Green Bay. She lived across the street from me, but was a few years older. At the age of 10 my mom wanted someone to watch me, but I was able to take care of myself. This is where Kathy came in. She would come over while my mom worked, usually Kathy's boyfriend would come over and we would swim most of the day. It was a win-win situation. Little did I know she would be a lifelong BFF.

Years later I was out to dinner with my husband and ran into her father. He tried to explain where she lived but I just wasn't familiar with the area enough to understand. He told me they lived in the same town as we did and that she was married with eight, yes I said eight kids. This narrowed down the search a bit.

A couple of weeks later my husband came home from the tavern, of course, and said he thinks he knows where my friend lives. At first I didn't know what he was talking about. Then he explained he saw a family with a pile of kids and he would take me there if I wanted.

The next day we piled the kids in the car and went out to eat at a near-by bar and grill. After eating, we stopped about a mile from there and I saw Kathy and her husband ready to take the kids and the dogs for a walk.

I jumped out of the car. Barely waiting for the car to stop and said. *"Kathy, Janet."* She said, *"No, Kathy."* I just laughed. It started a great friendship between her and me, our husbands and our children.

After one of my treatments Kathy was going to drop me off at home. At first when I got the treatments I stayed at Kathy's and she would tuck me in bed and I would watch movies or sleep. I probably hold the record for watching a movie for the first time, over and over again. I still have movies in the wrappers because I forgot I bought them. We would stop at Walmart on the way home and I would buy another movie. Not realizing I already had that one. You would have thought Kathy would have caught on though.

We learned the only way to survive was to use humor. My girlfriend's husband used to say that they were using subliminal messages to make me the next uni-bomber. Of course he was kidding. I think.

Kathy would say, *"You're so lucky, it is like sleeping with a different guy every night or being a virgin all over again."* Well that didn't last long. Besides it was difficult to sleep with my husband because of the picc line. And that was the last thing on our minds.

After a while, they gave me a little more freedom. Craig had to take my car keys away after a learning experience I had picking up the kids from school. We had one hair-raising experience on a day I had an ECT. It happened to be a day I had to take the neighbor kid home. Needless to say, his mother still doesn't like me. Let's just say, the kids were a bit shaken not stirred.

I drove like I was drunk. First I was on one side of the road, then on the other side of the road. I would be driving about 30 mph and then about 90 mph. Now I see why you're not supposed to drive on the same day you have a Shock Treatment! My phone was also monitored because I would call my mom and sister to let them know I was ok. With past treatments I would call them every 10 minutes to let them know I was ok because of the short term memory loss. I guess that isn't the end of the world, but I would get worried when I couldn't reach them. After the third call they started screening their calls. This got a little tiresome on their part. So Kathy would call them after the treatment to let them know I was ok and my phone was kept captive.

After another ECT, we had just gotten to our driveway and there was a Sheriff at the door.

"Mrs. Novitski"
"Yes"

"We got a call that your cows were out and wandering on the highway."

I was so confused, I didn't know what he was talking about, and why was he bothering me with this. Kathy explained to me that the cows were Craig's and they had to get the hired hands from the neighboring farm to put the cows away.

"You're going to have to get help from the neighbors, I just had shock treatment and I have to go lay down."
I went directly to the house, shut the door and left the officers in shock and with something useful to do as I laid down and forgot all about it. Later that week my sister in law called and was laughing about the cows getting out. Again I didn't know what she was talking about because of the memory loss. She had found out about the cows getting out from her parents that have a police scanner.

Actually, it is amazing at how much your neighbors and community helped out while this is going on.

I tried going to my son Erik's wrestling tournaments and Brian's basketball, but I was so out of it and didn't even know where I was. Erik's coach even let Erik follow the team bus to the tournament with my car so I could go to. Too bad I don't remember. That is when they started going themselves. The coach would bring Erik home from practice every night and the team bus would drop him off at the house after the tournament. That is one thing about living in a small community. They look after their own.

I felt so bad for the kids. They shouldn't have to go through this too. They had to grow up fast.
Erik was very athletic, so he was featured in the paper several times. At one point the reporter turned the story into a sob story about what he went through dealing with my illness instead of his talents or the teams talents. He focused on Erik taking me to shock treatments and what a wonderful son he was for taking his mother to shock treatments, going to school and being a star football player.

This was about the time they were in the playoffs and the team was angry with him because the story was all about him, instead of the team. They were not real forgiving and I feel it jeopardized the game. There wasn't much Erik could do about the story. I was embarrassed for my sons because basically anyone who didn't know about the shock treatments did now. Now our whole small town knew. Not everyone was as understanding about the bipolar.

At first I thought of myself as a laughing stock and an embarrassment to the kids. It took me awhile to accept my illness and who I was. Now I am open about my illness and my experiences hoping it will help someone else. Most people do not understand mental illness and are ignorant to the silent pain. Many people don't even look at it as a disease. But in most cases it is hereditary, passing it from one generation to the next.

Another incident Kathy brought me home and as she stepped in the door and I lunged at her.

"What the fuck is this?" I screamed.

There was a puppy. Kathy had given me a puppy a few months before. I didn't realize that it was our dog! I later accepted that the dog was ours, but I soon found a different home for Queenie because I just couldn't take care of her. I could barely take care of myself. The kids were very upset. I found a good home for her, but I still cried when she left.

I called my sister and bitched about the dog that Kathy had left there. Again and again I called.

"Kathy left one of her dogs here and she wouldn't take it back." After the shock, it became a great story for my family and friends. The doctor must have put a little extra juice in that treatment. Sorry sarcasm, again. This is one of the incident I don't remember. Everyone else did. Everyone was in disbelief that I could forget a dog that we had for six months. I was also in disbelief.

At one point Kathy had a conflict with the time of the ECT's; so she asked me if I could find other arrangements. So I called my nephew Jeremy. I knew he was off on Tuesdays and he and his wife decided to make a day of it. I don't know what they were thinking.
After my treatment, Jeremy and his wife Jessie thought they would take me to lunch and a movie. A very sweet gesture. One problem. I was so out of it that I barely ate

and then there was the problem of remembering the movie.
I didn't.

A couple of months later we were at my mom's to celebrate
Christmas, and a movie came on. *"This looks good"* I
say.

*"Janet, you already saw it. That's the movie you came to
with Jess and me."* Like I said it was a sweet gesture.
I went through another series of ECTs with the same
doctor. I wasn't allowed to talk to him before or after the
treatment. I had to go through my regular psychiatrist. He
didn't even ask how the treatments were going or about the
memory loss. He definitely did not care about his
patients. You could tell.

Later I found his treatments to be inhumane and
unethical. My following doctor did too after reading the
reports against my first doctor.

Chapter 5

Between my third and fourth series of ECTs, I was struggling, but wanted to try it without doing the shock treatments. I had heard that there was a day program that the hospital had. I ran into a girl who had been having trouble with life to put it lightly. She told me about the hospitals treatment program. Let's just say I was intrigued. I decided what could I lose. I talked to Dr. Hunter about it my very next visit. We both thought it would be a good idea. Actually I don't know why we didn't think of it before.

In an extreme case of depression, anxiety, bipolar disorder, substance abuse, or other behavioral health disorder, you may be encouraged to participate in a day treatment program. This is an intensive program that involves all-day, every day treatment and therapy over a specific period of time. This could include individual or group therapy. We also had classes on how to change our way of thinking. But most of all I enjoyed music therapy. This was very beneficial for me.

Treatment is tailored specifically for the individual; in this case it was for me. For example, if you're suffering from addiction issues, you'll work with certain therapists trained in dealing with substance abuse. You'll learn what triggers your addiction or your behaviors, and how you can develop different habits to change and overcome your dependency on drugs or alcohol or to deal with your mental health problems.

During treatment I learned that the people in your life and your surroundings can have significance in how you feel about yourself. Your surroundings can be anything from dishes in the sink to a family member who is abusive. When talking about your surroundings you have to first be aware of your personal boundaries and the people in your life. As you talk with your family and friends really evaluate if these are positive influences.

On more than one occasion I had to restrict my time with loved ones or be able to say *"NO"* if need be. When we think of boundaries, we think of a fence or a wall. But what about personal boundaries? The purpose of having boundaries is for protection. We need to be able to tell

people when they are acting in an unacceptable
manner. We need to be able to say NO!

The first step is to realize we have the right to protect
ourselves. Not only do we have a right, but a responsibility
to ourselves. Both mentally and physically. It is important
in any relationship to let others know how we feel. The
object is to do so without blaming. Let them know how
you feel. You may just open up some doors leading to
some great relationships.

There are many negative people or people in negative
situations. You may have to restrict time spent with these
people. In order to create a positive environment or mental
attitude may be beneficial to limit contact if the boundaries
you set for yourself are not being respected. I had to do this
with my friend Kathy. When she was going through her
divorce, I limited my time spent with her.

Although I did not have an addiction to drugs or alcohol,
many bipolar people do. They seem to medicate
themselves with the drugs and alcohol living in denial. I
knew many people like this.

Motivation can feel like an all or nothing experience. One moment is strong and the next you're questioning your very existence. Setbacks are a part of everyday life. Setbacks such as loss, failure and rejection can make us feel disappointed, frustrated or even sad. Your inner voice may be saying, *"How could you think you're good enough?* or *"You messed up again-what's new?"*

It is amazing how we self-talk. If someone else said these things to you, you'd argue back. But when our minds get the best of us we don't even question them. There's no magic formula for dealing with hard times, but you can start to recognize negative, self-defeating thoughts and stop them in their tracks.

Be prepared for setbacks, they are inevitable. When you get into a low, the faster you analyze it the better. Setbacks can make us anxious or depressed. Find ways to change your mood. Use your senses. Your senses carry funny pictures of family, friends, or pets. You can even put them on your keychain. They have the picture key chains anywhere from $10-$50. Put the pictures in a book or on your phone or mp3 player. Have your favorite songs ready. Scream if it makes you feel better.

I have a stack of DVD's next to my tv that always change my mood, even temporarily. Young Frankenstein, Rat Race, See Spot Run, Something about Mary, or a good Monty Python movie. I also have a stack of books. Sometimes it is hard to concentrate when you are in a downward spiral and this is why movies worked best for me.

Make a playlist of upbeat songs that you can listen to when you're down. Have it prepared ahead of time. You don't have to have a $200 Ipod. You can have a mp3 that you can get for $20 at Family Dollar or Big Lots. Get a couple and have them around. Make several playlists for variety. I learned this in music therapy.

There's a growing field of health care known as Music Therapy, which uses music to heal. Those who practice music therapy are finding a benefit in using music to help cancer patients, children with ADD, and others, and even hospitals are beginning to use music and music therapy to help with pain management, to help ward off depression, and for many other benefits that music and music therapy can bring. This is not surprising, as music affects the body and mind in many powerful ways.

I actually use music therapy while I am working out. It is amazing how the pain can be dulled by a favorite song. Sometimes this is the only thing that will get me through it.

Research has shown that music with a strong beat can stimulate brain waves to resonate in sync with the beat. Faster beats can bring sharper concentration and make you more alert, while a slower tempo will promote a calming effect, like a meditative state. Also, research has found that the change in brainwave activity levels that music can bring can also enable the brain to shift speeds more easily on its own as needed, which means that music can bring lasting benefits to your state of mind, even after you've stopped listening.

Music can help you get 'into the zone' when practicing yoga, self-hypnosis or guided imagery. It can also help you feel more energized when exercising, or help dissolve the stress when you're soaking in the tub, and be a helpful part of many other stress relieving activities. It can take an effective stress reliever and make it even more effective! Among the first stress-fighting changes that take place when we hear a tune is an increase in deep breathing. The body's production of serotonin also accelerates when listening to music. Choose music with a slow rhythm - slower than the natural heart beat which is about 72 beats per minute to help relax. Music that has repeating or cyclical pattern is found to be effective in most people for stress.

You can change your mood by changing the music you play for example. Here is a way to use music to wash away the blues. Select 3-4 songs which you feel are sad songs. Then select another 3-4 songs that makes you feel moderately more positive, slowly energizing than your present mood. Finally, select 3-4 songs that reflect the mood you would like to be; more confident, energized, and positive.

In other words, arrange the music so that it begins by reflecting how you feel right now, then arrange your selections in a progressive sequence to a mood that reflects how you would like to feel. This can be done ahead of time. This can be fun to do. Some people have hundreds of songs. See what kind of music lists you can come up with. Put the songs on an mp3 player or your phone. Be prepared. You can do this with any emotion, from anxiety to depression.

Also, you may want to be aware of the lyrics. Look at the song Bohemian Rhapsody. You can rock out to the beat of the music, but did you ever listen to the lyrics; quite negative.

I also learned to meditate. Sometimes this is the only thing that will slow down my mind. My mind opens up to new ideas and invigorates me. I try to do this at least a couple times a week. Meditation goes back over 4,000 years with over 200 different techniques. That's why you may have to experiment to find which one works best for you. Through meditation you can develop a lasting inner peace & happiness that does not depend on the outer world. Words will always fail to describe the inner experience of meditation. Some people call it meditation and some may call it prayer.

There are many different types of meditation, but ultimately they all share the common goal of quieting the mind and stopping our thoughts. When we meditate we must not allow either good or bad thoughts to enter the mind. No matter how illumining our thoughts are, meditation aims to give us a consciousness far beyond the domain of the intellect and our reasoning mind. By definition, words will always fail to describe the inner experience of meditation. Meditation can never be grasped by the finite intellectual mind; meditation deals with consciousness and a state of being. To understand meditation, we have to practice & experience it for ourselves.

Regardless, all meditation is effective in reducing stress and is being used more & more in the medical profession.

I actually was doing well after the outpatient treatment. I went a couple of years with only medication. But I had to

work on it. I got up the same time every day. I took my
medication every day at the same time. I learned not to
take naps or I wouldn't sleep at night. I saw my counselor
every week. I stayed away from alcohol. I saw my
psychiatrist regularly and I exercised.

I found alcohol actually made me depressed. Not just a
little bit, but for days. I would be either melancholy or
bitchy. Either way I did not like the outcome. I was not in
control of my attitude and the kids hid if they knew I had
alcohol.

I designed my first website around the outpatient
program. It is called *Ourpositiveworld.com*. I learned
through therapy to have a plan of action for when you get
depressed or even when you are manic. Our positive world
is full of funny movies, great songs, and great books.;
basically to keep the negativity out of my life. I know I
don't need it. I'm sure you don't either. Sorry sarcasm.

I also got to see the doctor a couple of times a week to
adjust my medication. This is when they put me on
Abilify. I was in heaven. I ended up going manic for a few

days. What is better than that? I finished a quilt in 3 days
and my house was spotless.

I learned to stay away from negativity. I cleaned house and
not in a literal way. I had to give up friendships that I had
for years.

I have a problem. I seem to feed off of others energy. If
someone is upset, I will be upset all day. Kathy and her
husband were going through a divorce and she was angry
for a better word. As well as she should be. But I had to
protect myself and limit my time with her.

I am also very emotional. I seem to feel other peoples
pain. Every year St. Jude's does a telethon on our local
radio station. I know it is a great cause and I donate to it
every year, but i can't listen to the testimonials that go on
all day. I can't. I realize this about myself and soon you
will learn your triggers.

Setting personal boundaries is a must when living a
positive lifestyle. It may feel uncomfortable at first, but it

helps to define you and what you are willing to put up with in your life.

If we don't know what boundaries are we probably don't have them, or we probably aren't conscious of when we are using them? We also do not know when someone is stomping over them or when we are stomping over someone else's boundaries.
When talking about boundaries you need to look at five different levels.

Physical, Mental, Emotional, Spiritual, and Behavioral.

PHYSICAL/SEXUAL BOUNDARIES may include hugging, touching. This is your responsibility to let others know when you feel uncomfortable. Maybe someone is just in your space. Maybe, you feel it is inappropriate to kiss in public. These are values that need to be shared. *"NO MEANS NO",* fits into this category.

MENTAL BOUNDARIES are your thoughts, ideas, and perceptions. Your likes and dislikes are what make you unique. It is ok to be different. Remember we must respect others beliefs. Stand your ground.

EMOTIONAL BOUNDARIES are how you feel. You have a right to have certain feelings about things. Even, strong feelings. Your feelings serve to protect you. You are allowed to have your feelings without others minimizing them. You gain great strength in your emotions and mental health each time you stand up for yourself and protect your emotional well-being. If someone crosses your emotional boundaries, you may choose to address the issue outright and work toward a mutual understanding, or you may decide to quietly set your boundary through limiting your time with that person or being involved in a particular situation. You may also find removing yourself from a toxic environment is necessary. This even means family.

BEHAVORIAL is being conscious of your actions. Remember you are responsible for your actions as well as the decisions you make. This may include other peoples boundaries. Be respectful. You can't make someone like you.

SPIRITUAL is whether you believe in a higher being. No one has the right to tell you what to believe in. Spirituality speaks through intuition, imagination as well as thoughts and feelings. As you pursue your spiritual growth, you will know your truth in your heart. Love, kindness, generosity, and healthy support for your fellow man will become part of your life as you experience your inner power, joy and peace. Setting boundaries in your spiritual life includes making time to pray, meditate, or even getting involved with causes dear to your heart.

Changing your thoughts can also help. A way of changing our thinking is to repeat affirmations throughout the day. Affirmations are a way of changing negative thoughts and feelings into positive ones. These short sentences are should be repeated with conviction and feeling.

Positive affirmations guide you into what you want to be true. This will bring you to your goals and desires. The stronger the emotion and feeling you put into your affirmations, the more powerful the results. You may want to write your affirmations down and put them next to your mirror or workspace. Repeat them a couple times a day if need be.

Affirmations can be said anytime of the day. You can be driving, mowing the lawn or even when you wake up or going to bed. The key is belief. KNOW it is true. BELIEVE it is fact. Use affirmations that you can believe in your heart and soul.

Designing *OurPositiveWorld.com* helped me build my self-esteem. I didn't think I could do it. But I did. It's not great, but it has had over 60,000 visitors. Nothing wrong with that. I had to teach myself how to design a website. Even learning what widgets are. (programs inside the website.) It was like I had to learn a different language.

I started seeing a counselor, Jan. She was just what I needed. This is her mission statement...A Lighthouse is the symbol of my mission statement "to provide a safe harbor and a guiding light of HOPE". May I offer you that safe harbor and guiding light of hope as you find your compass in life and navigate to calmer water's.

I took this literally. In high school I was class artist. I was always painting something, but after I got married and had children and I put this aside. After my first meeting with Jan I painted the picture on the cover of the book. Mind you I had not painted in some 20 years. I did this painting within three hours. Not too bad if I have to say it myself. For some reason I was driven to show her what I saw in my head.

The boat represents the depression that I suffer from and the lighthouse gives me hope. I guess I couldn't say it any better than that.

Chapter 6

Life wasn't just about downers. When I was up, I was really up. I remember making a rock garden the entire perimeter of my house. I would go out to the cow yard with a little red wagon and pick rocks, bringing them back to the house to put into place. Meanwhile my husband put a couple of piles of manure by the house that we spread out with a rake. The garden got bigger and bigger; beautiful but big.

Do you know how hard it is to keep up with the weeds. I do not have green thumb so now the rock garden is pretty much weeds. It was much more fun building the rock garden then to maintain it. Maybe I should eventually plant some flowers. Right now I have tiger lilies, hostas, and weeds.

My kids loved this. Guess who had to help with the spreading of the manure and get the rocks? They found other things to do rather quickly. I must have worked on that garden for over a week.

I also had times when I would go days without sleep or sleep very little. I can usually go about three to four days with very little sleep, but after that I am extremely emotional. I would cry at the drop of a hat. I even tiled the dining room floor at two in the morning. That was another experience to chalk up to mania.

Other hard times would include when I was working for my brother. He said I had two modes. I was either up high or down low. But, when I was high my sales were fantastic.

I have lost many friends in the years, not always sure what I did. Maybe it was because I didn't answer the phone every time they called. Most just couldn't handle the ups and downs. When you are sick though, you find out who your true friends are. When my medication isn't working I would get very argumentative or I was always right. Some are just embarrassed with mental illness.

I had a friend who called herself my BFF. When things got rough she went running. I miss having close friends. Sometimes I think they feel they have to keep their distance to protect themselves. I can see why they wouldn't want to be close to someone who is suicidal. When I became suicidal it was instantaneous. One minute I was fine the next I would be suicidal again. I wish I could be a little more technical to put some of you at ease, but it is a chemical imbalance that is for the most part hereditary.

For years I didn't know where the bipolar was coming from. Then I spent a summer with my father. He gets very little sleep and lives by the seat of his pants. Always having a way to make it rich. He also has a hard time hanging onto money. (This is also hereditary. I seem to have the same problem.) He doesn't seem to get suicidal; maybe because he goes to church twice on Sunday's.

You could say that I have depression on both sides of the fence, never realizing that my grandmother had trouble with depression. My father's mother had bouts of depression and did self-mutilation when stressed. My father also does this when he gets stressed. He picks and picks at his arms causing scabs. Picks the scabs and then scars his arms. He doesn't even realize he does it.

As I became more open about my illness, family members came out of the woodwork sharing their experiences with depression. It was amazing at how deep the depression ran. At least I feel that my family is a little more educated and accepting.

Chapter 7

My third series of ECT's was done by another doctor than
the previous two series of ECT's. I was doing pretty well
until the death of my sister's husband. I got a phone call
around 9 am and it was Lori. *"The police just left, Louie
was in an accident. I'm going to the hospital, I need you
here."* I put down the phone and got to work trying to find
a flight to Phoenix on short notice. I don't know how we
managed it, but I was there by 10pm.

At the time my sister called she had no idea what had
happened until she got to the hospital. She soon found out
Louie had a brain aneurysm and they had him on life
support. My niece Cassie picked me up at the airport and
we went to the house. There wasn't much I could do that
night.

The only problem was that we didn't have a key. Lori had
a six foot block fence. I couldn't believe that between my
23 year old niece and myself I was the one who scaled the
fence. If I haven't mentioned it before. I was not in great
shape. I don't even know how I was the one chosen to scale

the six foot fence. So I climbed the fence just to find the doors and windows were locked. I had to get in through the dog door and let Cassie in thru the garage. I was not happy. What a long day.

In the morning Lori was home, but she was leaving for the hospital so I hurried and went with. She had to inform Louie's family and a decision had to be made of Louie's outcome. It took about a week to get his family together and make the decision that it was best to let Louie rest in peace. I really did feel this was the right decision for him. He would have never wanted to live in a bed on a respirator.

They pulled the plug, so to speak, but he didn't fade away right away. He hung on. Lori had an appointment and had to leave for a while. That left my mom and I to watch over Louie. So I was holding Louie's Hand and my mom excused herself to the restroom. I was holding his hand and watching the monitor. It seemed like a millisecond and he flat lined. My mom came back and said *"what's wrong"*. All I could do was point to the monitor as the tears rolled down my face. He was gone.

I really did feel that he did this on purpose. You hear about this all the time, loved ones waiting for the right moment to pass away. Let me explain. The previous Christmas we had a party at my mom's in Wisconsin. Lori and Louie came from Phoenix. So did Lori's two sons, Jeremy and Mitch. Louie was not a fan of Mitch and he made it clear to him and everyone else. Mitch owed Louie money or something.

Louie had been drinking since 7 am, and by the time hell broke loose it was 10 pm. Louie went on a tangent and wanted to leave and get a hotel room. I told Lori she was not to get in that car with him. He told me, *"Shut up, you're just a psycho anyway, what do you know?"* How come when someone who is drunk there true feelings come out? I had always gotten along with him up to this point. He was drunk. I should be more understanding, but I'm not. Anyway we were not on the greatest terms at this point. This was in December and he had his accident in April.

In the meantime Lori was on her way back and we stopped her in the hall to tell her what happened. We left her to say her goodbyes. She had a lot of decisions to make about Louie's organs and arrangements. She chose to have him cremated and had not one, but two ceremonies.

This was extremely hard on me, let alone my sister. I had never really lost anyone close to me, let alone losing someone while you watched. I had never experienced anything close to death and I didn't exactly handle it very well. By my forties I had only been to four funerals. I know this is probably not normal. By the time I got home I needed to have shock treatments again.

While I was going through my ECT's my sister met someone. Only a few short weeks after her husband died. I know you don't have a choice of when you meet someone, but I felt she never mourned the death of her husband and still struggles with it today. In the meantime I was not thrilled about going through the ECT's while she was screwing around with her new boyfriend. I will tell you that she is still with him. The timing just wasn't right.

When I got home I scheduled an appointment with Dr.
Hunter and we started making arrangements for my third
set of ECT's. I had been to many psychiatrists in the past.
But, Dr. Hunter was by far more superior then the other
doctors I had seen. He was younger than most of the
doctors, but he was smarter also. He was always looking
for something better out there to help with mental
illness. He did the shock treatments with minimal memory
loss. He cared about his patients and their outcome.

When I saw him for the very first times he surprised me
when he asked me, "Just how much is your family willing
to let you feel?" In other words can we adjust your
medications so that you are allowed to have
feelings. Otherwise doctors try to medicate you until you
are numb.

I started with Dr. Hunter when my other doctor had
retired. I was not real excited about him treating me
because he was the one who bitched me out after my
suicide attempt. But I sucked it up. Another reason I
started seeing him was because was one of the few who
could actually perform the ECT treatments.

He also says it like it is… This is good thing, because I do
to. He didn't sugar coat anything he was going to do. He
is also not afraid to swear. One time I was in his office and
I hear him say, "This fucking computer." The hospital had
gotten a new program and he wasn't a fan.

He had promised things would be different than my
previous treatments. I would suppose anything would be
better. My treatments were at a different hospital and
although I don't remember much after the treatments, I do
remember the first treatment.

I was led into a private room separated with glass. The
nurse took my vitals and made sure I was comfortable by
giving me a warm blanket. I wish I had that at home. My
anxiety was high. I was afraid to go under one more time. I
hated the feeling of going under and this was effecting me
trying to fall asleep. I kept seeing the mask going over my
face. I could even smell the plastic from the mask. Just the
smell of plastic would give me an anxiety attack.

The anesthesiologist came in to check my allergies and to
tell me what was going to happen. By then Dr. Hunter had

arrived and told the nurses that there would only be three people in the room to avoid anxiety. Although I was grateful it really didn't help. The gesture was nice. I was very thankful for this.

The anesthesiologist was about to administer the medication for me to sleep when I got an anxiety attack . Then my numbers were elevated. Dr. Hunter didn't even flinch. He just told him to wait just a few minutes for me to calm down. The nurse took my hand and held it as I was going under.

By this time I was becoming an expert. All I needed was a driver to take me home. And I would rest the rest of the day. Mostly sleeping, but I did throw in a movie now and then. Usually one I haven't seen, but really I had seen it probably fifty times. On the upside the ending was always new to me. If you couldn't tell one of my favorites was Young Frankenstein. I loved this movie, but the kids were getting sick of it. I have kind of a warped sense of humor.

The hard part of this was my sixteen year old son had to pick me up and go to school after he drove me home. I know it was hard on him. I felt helpless because not only was I going through this, but my family was going through it too. This was affecting his school work.

This is one of the reports I found from my son Erik's junior year. It ripped my heart. Sorry in advance for some of the repeated stories. I left it as is because it is a little late to correct his spelling and grammar. Also some of the stories may be repeated.

Mom

I am a seventeen year old momma's boy. I have been helping my mom cope with her problems for years. My mom has severe depression and bipolar. To anyone who knows what these two disabilities are you would know how painful it is to her. Most people can deal with these problems through medication but she is a rare case. She is one of the two percent that happens to tolerate medicine, this means that her meds will work at first, but then her body seems to become immune. Throughout years of different medicines I don't think there is one antidepressant out there that she hasn't tried.

*Her doctors have come down to no other choice but
to give her ECT's. ECT's are Electric shock treatments.
The doctors take two suction cups connected to a generator
and then stick them to your head. The electricity will
release a chemical in your brain. That chemical is what
triggered her disabilities. I was the one who drove my mom
weakly to the hospital for her treatments. Mostly because
my step dad works constantly and isn't home often and I
am the only other one with a license. I soon found out that
it gave her memory loss. At first it was just small things,
then it came to not remembering what happened yesterday,
then a weak, then she couldn't remember what happened
for an entire month.*

*It was my first year on varsity wrestling, and my coaches
understood her situation and let me drive her to my
tournaments instead of riding with the team. She could only
stay in the gym so long without feeling nauseous or get
migraines. She had to stop coming all together. Losing
support from one of the closest person to me was very hard
and I felt alone. All together my mom's memory was getting
shorter and shorter. The two months she was going through
her shock treatments she can't remember. She had lost two*

full months of her memory that she will never get back. She couldn't even remember that I was wrestling.

We also had gotten a puppy for her right before she had stated the treatments to keep her company. We had the puppy for over six weeks and it was one of the only things that made her happy. After her 4th treatment she came home and yelled "who's dog is this, get it out right now!" I was confused and didn't know what to do. I told her it was her puppy and we've had it for a while. But she insisted that we didn't and ended up giving the puppy to a new home.

In these few months she forgot about my wrestling, a puppy, and my birthday. She didn't know what was happening in her daily life and she was in pain twenty four hours of the day. Her days were spent sitting on the couch recuperating from the seizures the treatment gave her. Many People believe this lifestyle is inhumane and unnatural. It is sad to say that this treatment is the only thing that is keeping her from keeping sane.

I think it was hardest on the kids. It is not easy having a parent with mental illness. As far as the kids were, they had to grow up fast and I think they resent it. But I was lucky. I have great kids who also are sympathetic to others. Between my third and fourth series of ect's I chose medication. Erik was a senior this year and playing football and wrestled. The medication made me dizzy and I slept a lot but I wanted to remember his senior year. What a year it was. He was an all-star athlete breaking two high school records in football.

I sat with my ex mother in law so she could translate the game. Someone usually had to take my arm as I walked up the bleachers so I didn't fall, but all in all I made it. I just had to suffer through the medication.

Brian was having a hard time in school. Always getting teased and bullied, pretty much since the fourth grade. He was bullied most by his so called friends. It seemed like I was at the school every other week trying to find a solution.

It was about the time he was sixteen we found out he had bipolar and ADHD. Although,,I suspected. He would come up with these fantastic ideas. He is very intelligent. The next minute he would be crying saying he hated his life. Nothing rips at a mother than to see your child in pain and not be able to do anything about it. I could relate, but everyone suffers differently. He was no different.

We took him in to see a doctor who put him on Lamictal and another drug for the ADHD, but he didn't like the way it made him feel. She was reluctant to put him on anything else. I think because of her in experience. When he was closer to 18 he stopped taking the drugs all together. We watched him closely. Mainly we had to make sure he got enough sleep or there was no reasoning with him. He became very emotional with the lack of sleep; also argumentative.

If two people could clash it was him and me. I don't know if we are to much the same or too different. All I know is that I wish I could take back the pain I caused him. He definitely did not respect me. This was hard. He just blew off anything I said and I did not have the support of his father to reason with him. It was almost like they both were against me.

Chapter 8

I should have known I was going to crash and burn, but I was ignoring the signs. In fact, I missed all the signs. Basically I think It would been easier if someone stood in front of me naked with a sandwich board; saying, "Get Help!" It wasn't until I started living with the repercussions of my actions during the weeks I was manic.

During this time I started a business called Suddenly Bubbles. I started buying melt and pour soap without propylene glycol, or titanium dioxide. Then I started making whipped body butter and sugar scrubs. I had one speed and it was go, go, go. I was like a machine getting my products ready; literally, day and night.

I created an awesome logo. I formed an LLC. Made labels and bought the ingredients to finish making the products. Suddenly Bubbles was formed.

Homemade soaps and Gifts

suddenly bubbles

I was also getting ready for the big grand opening that was going to be in the office of our garage. I had to remove everything that was thrown in the room for the past ten years. Painted it and cleaned the floors. Picking out the perfect colors, I made curtains to cover all the windows. I even made sure I had all the legal papers to start such a business. Next I made a website and I also put items on etsy.com. I was in business.

I bought a sign for my front yard, along with decorating around the sign with painted tires in different colors to make a garden. (I still haven't planted any flowers.) Then when everything was done, I had a ton of soap, and body products, that no one bought. Meanwhile, during this time I spent over $5000 in a month. Yes, a month. If this wasn't a clue, I don't know what is. I could go on, but I think you get the idea. I was definitely manic.

I always say, "what goes up must come down." It did. I started withdrawing and getting more and more depressed. And needless to say, my husband Craig was not happy about the money spent. Especially, since we needed a new roof for our 100 year old home. One clue should have been the shingles on the lawn, but you could say I wasn't a genius. I couldn't blame Craig for being angry. But at this point I couldn't do anything other than apologize and fall deeper in depression for what I had done.

My eldest, Michael, turned 23, and my youngest Brian, graduated High School all in the same week. I was getting older and the kids were getting older. I knew I was sliding then but I couldn't do anything about it. I knew things were going to change, and it would be just Craig and I.

The night before Brian's graduation, he wanted to go out to dinner to celebrate his graduation. I called Craig, but no answer. This meant one thing. HE WAS IN THE TAVERN. I must have called for hours when Brian finally went to bed. "That's ok. I am use to it," he said as he headed up the stairs to go to bed. Those words cut like a knife. It was bad enough that I dealt with Craig's drinking, but I didn't realize how it affected the kids or at least I had the delusion that the kids were not affected. It was like I shielded my eyes from seeing what was happening.

He came home about 9:30, my anger engulfed me. Screaming,"It's bad enough you do this to me, but now you are doing it to the kids." I turned on my heels and went up to bed crying. I should tell you that Craig got laid off that day, but I didn't care. Maybe a little communication would have been in order.

I was awakened to him bumping into the closet door. He had to go to the bathroom, but couldn't find the door that left the bedroom to the downstairs bathroom. I had to turn on the light. He was going to pee in the closet. Nice. It's not like he hasn't done that before. He then slept on the couch which was becoming more often than not.

The following day, Friday, was Brian's graduation and Craig stayed sober and was on his best behavior. I was so proud of Brian. He had struggled in High School and at one point wanted to drop out. He stuck it out and got his diploma. That night he stayed at the school lock in and the following night he had to work making it a little difficult to find the time to take him out for dinner. He worked on a neighboring farm as well as Craig.

Brian had been working on that farm since he was eight years old. He worked the bagging machine that they blew feed into. He worked for a farm that did custom bagging. By now he was driving semi for them and hauling feed and spreading manure at different times of the year.

On Sunday, I called Craig to tell him we should take Brian out to dinner for Graduation, but again he didn't answer the phone. I called for three hours until Brian told me to check out THE ROCKY TOP, a local tavern that he frequents. As I drove to the corner I saw Craig taking a friend home going in the opposite direction. So I decided to follow him. As he drove back towards me, I drove in his lane to make him stop. I wasn't really thinking that he may not stop, but that is another story. I instantly started screaming at him about how he is letting down his family. He ignored me and drove towards home. I was past angry. I was Irrational. I felt the pain of the past twenty years.

I got home, and stormed to him and went after him like a freight train. I was like a hurt animal. I charged him like a rhino and yes, I started hitting him. First in the face and he tried to restrain me while I was calling him a "FUCKING DRUNK." Not exactly the best way to handle the situation. I must have scratched him because he was bleeding. Later I regretted what I had done. He never hit me back, he stood his ground, but then walked away from the situation. We still took Brian out to dinner, but it was a quiet evening with us not talking to each other. Poor Brian.

I later apologized, but I knew that wasn't enough. I knew I had a problem. I never went after anyone like that.

Afterwards I just sobbed. I cried so hard I started to hyperventilate and had to vomit.

I had been without a Psychologist for about a year and a half. I was getting my medication from my family doctor, but he really didn't know much about psychiatric drugs. He had kept me on the same drugs that I started with. He was afraid to change them because of my history with other medications. I had been looking for a Psychologist, but they couldn't find one in my area that was in my network. I called the union hall monthly looking for a doctor. Boy they make it hard for mentally ill people just to get help.

I knew I was going to have to go inpatient, again! I just wanted to crawl in a hole and die. I called the insurance company again to get help, but they told me that day was my last day with their company. I started to panic and called the union hall to find out that they were switching to a new network. I was pissed. I was sick of running through hoops, but this actually worked out to my advantage.

They covered my old Psychologist, but he no longer took outpatients. Another road block. I called twenty five different doctors that were in my network, both in Appleton and Green Bay. The Psychiatrists told me I needed a doctors referral and there would be a wait of two months to a year. I had to have a doctor from their hospital give me a reference before I could be seen. They pretty much told me that the only way I could get the help I needed was to go inpatient.

All this happened on Friday, but I had my niece's graduation party on Sunday and my girlfriend needed a ride to Mayo for cancer treatment the next week so even though I Knew I was sliding there was nothing I could do about it. I was her last option to take her on the five hour drive to Mayo in Rochester on Tuesday, stay over, and come back Wednesday. This meant that the soonest I could go in was on Thursday. I was just going to have to wait.

I got through all of my prior engagements and Craig took me in. I started tearing up in the waiting room and when I was in the emergency room I had to tell the doctor that *"My medication isn't working and I don't want to hurt myself or anyone else.* " How degrading. I felt helpless. I did not want to be there, but what choice did I have.

This hospital was stricter than the previous hospital that I was inpatient at. As they checked me in they took blood samples to check my drug levels. I am a difficult draw, so it took five tries before they got enough blood. I was totally black and blue. They probably thought I did heroin too.

Meanwhile, they took all of my clothes and made me wear a gown until they had time to go through the clothes and luggage. This took a couple of hours because they had quite a few new patients. They had to look for any strings such as laces, or drawstrings. They also checked for drugs and anything you could harm yourself or others with. I couldn't even have my nook or Ipod. It was days before I got to use a pen. I had to use crayons. I was so excited just to have a pencil, but that took a while too.

It was embarrassing being the only one in the room wearing a gown. I was hoping nothing popped out. Before I had to go into group, the nurse gave me a tour and showed me to my room. Tears were just rolling down my face. We went past a room, where the door opened and I saw monitors with the view of every room. I was shocked, I never expected that. I didn't even have privacy using the bathroom. I had been inpatient two other times and they never did that. I was already feeling like my personal space was being violated and had .a lack of control. They had total control of what I did and when I did it. I felt like a child. Maybe robot was a better analogy.

The first night there was a young girl that started throwing things and acting out. I know she was there for help, but this did not help my anxiety. I could feel my body shaking. It felt like I couldn't escape the anxiety that was growing inside my body. I went to the nurses desk and asked for valium. Thank god the doctor had an order for the drug so that I could be relieved from the symptoms that continued to build. I just wanted to run.

The night security stayed by her room all night to keep her under control to no avail. The following day a nurse had to watch her by following her like ducklings follow its mother. They still had difficulty controlling her. She went from door to door slamming it making sure it was closed. Bang! Bang! Bang! Over and over again. Making me jump each time she slammed the door.

Again I took valium to get through it.

I saw the doctor for the first time that day. Again I saw Dr. Hunter. Because I had a history with him, they let me see him. In a way I was relieved, but I was also fearful that ECT's would be one of the number one ways to control my moods. I was thankful that he adjusted my meds and we decided to use ECT's as a last result. This immediately removed some of the anxiety I was experiencing. I can relate it to a student who just passed their finals.

I started seeing a new doctor that I wasn't really sure about, but I also continued seeing my counselor, Jan. She was amazing. My new doctor and I just didn't click the way Dr. Hunter and I did. Besides I was used to Dr. Hunter telling me like it is. If he felt something wasn't going to work, he made sure he blatantly told me until it got across.

Within a few months I was experiencing severe leg cramps and muscle tenderness. I was afraid of the side effects from Abilify. So I called my doctor and went in but he did not change any of my medications. In fact, he added another new drug that is supposed to help with muscle cramps. It caused slurred speech, it affected my eyesight, my mouth was so dry when I drank water I swear it did not even hit the back of my throat. Did you ever buy towels that actually repelled the water? It's like that.

I asked my psychiatrist if he thought I should try to do ECT's again. He wasn't really for them or against them. He never really had much to say. I felt it was time. I made it through December and most of January before I started getting out of control again. I thought if I went with the ECT's, I could actually get to maintenance ECT's, which would only be once a month. I could deal with that. But I knew the next month will be a roller coaster ride from hell. He set up an appointment with Dr. Hunter to talk with me about the ECT's.

By the following day I had a meeting with Dr. Hunter. I was nervous a bit, actually more than just a bit. All the memories from the previous ECT's flooded me. I actually went through counseling trying to deal with the side effects of memory loss and what that does to your family. It takes a lot out of you. I see the kid's heart sink every time they say. "Remember when?" This time I was bound and determined I would be prepared mentally and physically for this series of treatments.

Then I decided to look back at my situation and thought what were these medications doing to me. I have been on these so many different medications for over the past 20 years. Over the past two decades I have experienced high liver enzymes, slurred speech, weight gain, blurred vision, tremors, hair loss, dry mouth, rashes and my throat closing up so I couldn't breathe. What was I doing to my body? How many years will I be able to be on these drugs before they cause permanent damage?

Craig and I always made a joke about who's going to need the first liver transplant. It is a toss-up between him and me.

When I got to Dr. Hunter's office I met with him and he always has a way of settling your nerves. He really didn't need to explain a lot about the treatments. I knew what I was in for. But I told him I have to get my affairs in

order. He looked confused. This was not my first rodeo. I
needed to get all my paperwork together. I needed to get
our taxes done, and write down all my passwords and
decide how I was going to journal every day to make some
sense of what was going on. This was an idea from
previous treatments that seemed to work.

Before I left, I gave him two of the soaps that I made the
last time I was manic. When I went manic I started a
company called Suddenly Bubbles. He smelled the soaps
and asked, *"Did you do this?"* I replied with a yes, and
explained about going manic. He shook his head and said,
sometimes I don't understand you. *" Your mania is
borderline genius."* I didn't understand.

I think what he was trying to say was that my mind kept
going. I always had an idea. Good or bad.

I made notes everywhere. It didn't help me remember later
but at the time I was somewhat functional. I didn't notice
the memory loss until I was done with my treatments, but it
was hard on the kids.

They would win awards or have sporting events, and I wouldn't remember it and I never got those memories back. They also thought that I would forget about them. But most of all they used it to their advantage. If they asked me one night if they could do something, and I said no, they would ask the following night for a yes. All the time I didn't remember them asking me the night before.

A few days later I went in for a physical. They had no idea on what to do. They never had to do a physical for ECT's before. Then again the doctor looked like he just got out of school. Anyway I got all the lab work done and a required AKG. I will have to do this once a month to get the treatments. It is state law, at least in Wisconsin. I'm not sure of other states.

Now I wait. They need to check the results to see whether my body can handle the treatment. My time is getting closer and I am starting to get nervous. I know that I won't have control over anything for the next few weeks. Not only do you feel hopeless, but you feel helpless. More like a child. Now I hurry up and wait. I am waiting for the doctor's office to call to tell me when my appointment is for my Picc Line. It is not common for someone to need a picc line for ECT's , but the idea of 5-6 people trying to find a vein was the worst part of the ECT's. I would be in tears before the treatment even started, wondering if I was going to get electrocuted from my own tears. Not exactly a happy thought.

I was going to a different hospital this time. I decided to follow the doctor who had helped me several times over the years. First he was the one who gave me a huge lecture on the pain I would be giving my family if I was successful at suicide. Then he recommended the outpatient program in which I learned how to think positively. Most of all he felt that he could help me with the ECTs without having substantial memory loss.

It is important to note that if you are experiencing a lot of memory loss, there are alternatives to the electrodes than just the temples. Don't be afraid to get a different doctor either if you are uncomfortable. If I only knew during my first couple of series it would have been a lot easier on me.

I finally got my appointment and had to be there an hour before the doctor to prep for the treatment.

"Janet, we are ready." The nurse paged. *"Do you need the restroom?"*

I thought this might be a good idea, since I was going to lose all bodily functions and all. After, I was given privacy to undress and put on a gown. They had me in a private room this time I went before everyone else. Dr. Hunter knew the anxiety I had from previous treatments at the other hospital. So he always made sure I was first. I thought this was very considerate on his part. I crawled under the sheets of the nice warm blankets on the gurney. Then the nurse knocked.

The nurse hurried around to prep me for my ECT. Another knock at the door and the anesthesiologist came in to ask me some more questions and explain what was going to happen. I had so many treatments that just the smell of the mask that is put over your face for breathing would cause an anxiety attack. The anesthesiologist was very sympathetic and put lavender in the mask to help calm me down. It actually worked.

Dr. Hunter would only allow a nurse, the anesthesiologist and himself in the room for the procedure. They put bumper pad around the bed and Dr. Hunter talked to me about wrestling. I know it isn't a normal thing to talk about before a procedure like this, but whatever works, right? His kids were in wrestling and my son was in wrestling. This helped ease my anxiety. He started to put a pressure cuff around my calf. This was to monitor the seizure I was about to have. Dr. Hunter then started to put the electrodes on my forehead as they asked me to count backwards. The next thing I know I woke up in recovery.

I had to pay someone to take me to and from the appointments because they were in the middle of the day and I couldn't drive. So I waited for someone to pick me up. I was given some juice and toast while I waited. I was a little disoriented, but ecstatic that I had my memory. I could even remember the conversation I had Dr. Hunter before the procedure. It was amazing the difference between my first and second series from my third and fourth series of ECTs.

I went home and rested, took a nap, watched some tv and went to bed. Craig had pretty much given up on me by this time. Not even asking how the treatments went. He washed his hands of me. I think he is just tired of the fight. I know it is one thing that I have this fight every day not to do something stupid. But he has his own fight.

In the past ten years he has lost two very close friends to suicide and a wife who has been unsuccessful. This has got to do something to an individual. It wasn't long before I decided to stay with my sister in Phoenix because of the isolation and loneliness I felt. I ended up staying with her for two months. By then I was missing Craig and the kids.

ou do not get the wrong idea about this book. The
ifficult on my family and me but it was
ful. Without them I truly believe I
essful at one point with suicide. My
planning on ECT's is to plan on

some memory loss. Write things down. Be patient with
yourself.

The other thing that I want people to understand is that in
some cases, suicide is not planned. The mind works in
mysterious ways and suicidal thoughts can come in a flash;
without warning. I have spoken with other bipolar patients
and this happens often. It can be a beautiful day and the
next thing you know a cloud of darkness engulfs you and
you want to drive straight into a tree. Sometimes this could
be due to a medication change or the combinations of
medications. Regardless, there are times you are not in
control of your thoughts.

Just don't be afraid to get help. Bipolar is a disease and
should be treated as one. It is not an embarrassment. It is
not different than a person with diabetes or cancer.

We just have to be strong.

between my first and second series from my third and
fourth series of ECTs.

I went home and rested, took a nap, watched some tv and
went to bed. Craig had pretty much given up on me by this
time. Not even asking how the treatments went. He
washed his hands of me. I think he is just tired of the fight.
I know it is one thing that I have this fight every day not to
do something stupid. But he has his own fight.

In the past ten years he has lost two very close friends to
suicide and a wife who has been unsuccessful. This has got
to do something to an individual. It wasn't long before I
decided to stay with my sister in Phoenix because of the
isolation and loneliness I felt. I ended up staying with her
for two months. By then I was missing Craig and the
kids.

I hope you do not get the wrong idea about this book. The
ECT's were difficult on my family and me but it was
necessary and helpful. Without them I truly believe I
would have been successful at one point with suicide. My
advice to you if you are planning on ECT's is to plan on

some memory loss. Write things down. Be patient with yourself.

The other thing that I want people to understand is that in some cases, suicide is not planned. The mind works in mysterious ways and suicidal thoughts can come in a flash; without warning. I have spoken with other bipolar patients and this happens often. It can be a beautiful day and the next thing you know a cloud of darkness engulfs you and you want to drive straight into a tree. Sometimes this could be due to a medication change or the combinations of medications. Regardless, there are times you are not in control of your thoughts.

Just don't be afraid to get help. Bipolar is a disease and should be treated as one. It is not an embarrassment. It is not different than a person with diabetes or cancer.

We just have to be strong.